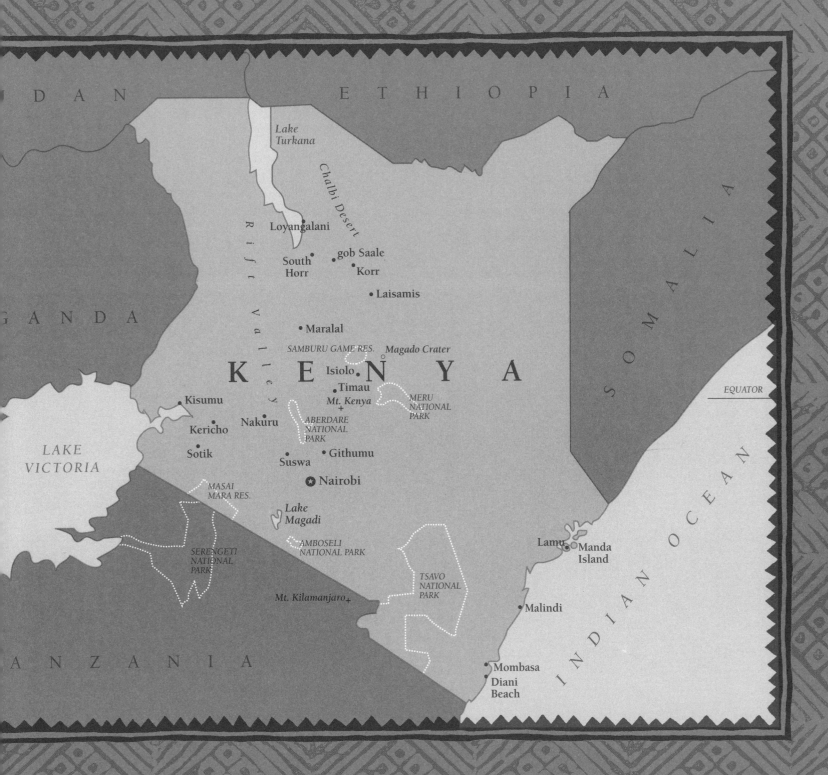

ETHIOPIA

SUDAN

Lake
Turkana

Chalbi Desert

Rift Valley

Loyangalani

South
Horr

gob Saale

Korr

• Laisamis

UGANDA

• Maralal

SAMBURU GAME RES.

Magado Crater

KENYA

SOMALIA

Isiolo

Timau
Mt. Kenya
+

MERU
NATIONAL
PARK

EQUATOR

Kisumu

Nakuru

ABERDARE
NATIONAL
PARK

Kericho

Sotik

Suswa

• Githumu

LAKE
VICTORIA

★ Nairobi

MASAI
MARA RES.

Lake
Magadi

SERENGETI
NATIONAL
PARK

AMBOSELI
NATIONAL PARK

TSAVO
NATIONAL
PARK

Lamu

Manda
Island

INDIAN OCEAN

Mt. Kilamanjaro +

TANZANIA

Malindi

Mombasa
Diani
Beach

All along I felt it was our destiny to go on the safari to Kenya. Neither of us had expectations to be met, so perhaps that made us more open to our Kenyan experience. I'm glad that I went with you - my dear friend - rather than a relative. That too made the experience deeper, for we only had to attend to ourselves rather than someone else. Of course will remember the incidents, such as the "thing" in your bed at Mt Kenya Safari Club which turned out to be a hot water bottle. But how can words explain what happened in our hearts & minds? You are the one person who will KNOW. May that stay with us forever - the effects of our remarkable journey.

Trish
07/07/99 - 07/21/99

For Barbie Allen
In memory of Galyago Segelan

Special thanks to Charles McCarry, Declan Haun,
Tom Kennedy, Kent Kobersteen, Elie Rogers,
Margaret MacLean, Larry Lucchino,
Virginia Miller, Njoroge and Susan Munoru,
Liz Davis, Bill Baker, James Malcolm,
and Elizabeth Brown.

(Page 1) Impalas, Masai Mara Reserve.
(This page) El Molo tribesman near Loyangalani.
(Pages 4-5) Lake Turkana.

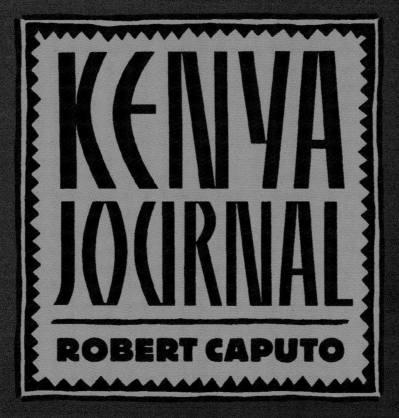

KENYA JOURNAL

ROBERT CAPUTO

ELLIOTT & CLARK PUBLISHING • WASHINGTON DC

INTRODUCTION

The roar of gas burners pierced the African dawn as the pilot pumped hot air into the enormous orange and yellow balloon. We rose above Keekerok Lodge and drifted out over the undulating grasslands of Kenya's Masai Mara Game Reserve. Zebras, gazelles, giraffes, and elephants grazed below, and a pride of lions finished off the night's kill. Then the burners were switched off, and we floated with the wind. There was no sound, no sensation of movement, not even the rush of air against my cheeks. It seemed more as if the earth were revolving slowly underneath.

In other parts of the Great Rift Valley, scientists have discovered abundant evidence of early man and his forebears. Suspended above the savannah, I sensed the timelessness of Africa. I could easily imagine a prehistoric family living there, competing with their fellow creatures for food.

But Kenya is not timeless. The European powers, when they divvied up Africa a century ago, coined the term "Kenyan" to describe the autonomous and often antagonistic tribal peoples who lived within the boundaries they drew. In fewer than three generations, these disparate groups have struggled to shape a modern nation. Few places on earth have faced such precipitous change, and few African countries have managed the process as well as Kenya. The more than 30 ethnic groups that comprise the country have so far avoided the interminable civil strife that plagues most of Kenya's neighbors.

The years of peace since independence in 1963 have allowed Kenya to develop rapidly; coffee, tea, and tourism money has gone to roads and services rather than guns. In fact, Kenya's most pressing problems are due to the headlong pace of its progress.

I've spent quite a bit of time in Kenya since I first went there in 1972, and been lucky enough, through friendships with various Kenyans and assignments for *National Geographic*, *Time*, *Life*, and other magazines, to have traveled through most of the country. Some parts have been altered dramatically since my first visit, others hardly at all, but everywhere I sense the imminence of change.

The Kenya of 50 years ago, the Kenya of Karen Blixen and Ernest Hemingway, is gone. And Kenya will be different 50 years from now. Traditional cultures and much of the wildlife must inevitably give way to the growing numbers of people and their embrace of homogenizing modern life.

The transformation is swift. I recently sat on the porch of an isolated mission hospital, watching a videotape with the patients, nomads from the surrounding countryside. The tape was of a wedding in one of their villages. A young man who had been away from his people for several years turned to me when the tape ended and said, "I never knew a lot of those things."

On these pages, I have sought to convey some of my impressions of Kenya at this moment in its history, when rhinoceroses and shopping malls, sorcery and biotechnology, camel nomads and stockbrokers coexist.

THE NORTHERN FRONTIER

The pavement ends at Isiolo. A spiked barrier lies across the road that continues, rough and dusty, through what was once known as the Northern Frontier District. I stopped the car and walked over to the guardhouse where a camouflage-clad policeman added my name and the license plate number to the list of every vehicle that enters or leaves the area. In recent years, there have been attacks along the road by *shifta*, Somali bandits who roam the region to the east.

Most foreigners passing through the barrier are headed for lodges and game drives 20 miles down the road in Samburu National Park, and are free to move on. I was going farther north and was told I would either have to wait for a convoy or carry an armed escort. I did not want to wait and be forced to keep pace with heavy trucks on the jolting corduroy road, so two policemen, bound for duty on the frontier and armed with old 303s, climbed into the car, and we set off.

Northern Kenya is wild, a great swath of harsh land that sweeps east from the Ugandan border to Somalia and south toward the coastal plain, an arc around the fertile central highlands. Water is scarce. The earth is largely stone and sand; vegetation ranges from thick bush and acacia woodlands to nothing. Countless seasonal streambeds called *lugga*s drain the region's meager rainfall but not into any lake or sea; they simply disappear into deserts.

The din of the car racing over the corrugations precluded much conversation with my escort. I stared instead along the white cut of road that stretched through miles of low, gray brush, at a horizon occasionally broken by mountains thrust up from the rocky earth.

A few tiny settlements clung to the road—just a couple of *duka*s (shops), a police post, some ragged huts, and sometimes

a small mission church. We passed herds of cattle being driven toward water by Samburu warriors. But mostly the landscape was empty.

Though humans are few in northern Kenya, their history is ancient. On the shores of Lake Turkana, scientists have discovered evidence of early man, including an almost perfect skeleton of *Homo erectus*, a hunter-gatherer who inhabited the area about 1.6 million years ago when it was less arid. In more recent times, only pastoral nomads have been capable of wresting sustenance from the region's grudging environment.

About 19,000 Rendille camel herders roam the area between the road and Lake Turkana, just south of the Chalbi Desert. Pastoral people tend to be more resistant to change than cultivators, and the Rendille are as little affected by the developments sweeping through modern Kenya as any group in the country. Schools, hospitals, roads—the signposts by which Westerners and westernized Africans define progress—are virtually nonexistent in their land.

The Rendille's portable huts are made by stretching hides and sisal mats over frames of lashed poles. Their diet is camel's milk, supplemented by goat's milk and meat. They grow no crops. The Rendille like tea, sugar, and the occasional bowl of *ugali* (cornmeal) recently available at *duka*s that have sprung up on the periphery of their territory. But they need the shops and their wares about as much as they need the national government; if the modern world were suddenly to disappear, the Rendille would get along just fine. "We don't really like that food of farmers," one Rendille elder told me. "The best thing is to feed a child only camel's milk until he is grown. That way he will be strong and fast."

I talked with this elder, whose name was Galyago, when I

Galyago and son milking camel, gob Saale. (Left) Rendille herdsman and camels near Korr.

11

Galyago and son.
(Right) Rendille woman
carrying firewood,
gob *Saale.*

visited his *gob* (village) with Liz Davis, a nurse and old friend who has lived in eastern Africa for several years, and Satim, a young Nairobi-educated Rendille we had picked up at a mission to translate for us; none of the people in Galyago's *gob* spoke English or even Swahili, the lingua franca of Kenya, a fact which underscores both their isolation and their contentment with life as it is and has been.

Galyago, whom Satim described as the "elder in charge of doing," immediately took us under his wing. He introduced us to the other elders at a meeting called to greet us, where he divvied up the sugar, tea, and chewing tobacco we had brought as gifts, and he helped us make camp beneath a tall acacia at a nearby *lugga*. Several elders and a gaggle of children gathered to watch. Galyago pitched right in, grabbing a rock to drive pegs into the ground, stretching guy wires tight, then crawling into the tent to have a look. In fact, Galyago seemed eager to try whatever came along. None of the others had any desire to taste our food, but Galyago tried oranges, which he liked, potatoes and beans, which he didn't, and carrots, which he spat out in disgust. "This is not food," he declared.

That first day, after Liz and I had gamely swallowed several mugs of the almost sickeningly rich camel's milk Galyago gave us, he showed us around the *gob*, a circle of domed huts on the vast plain of baked earth and desert scrub. Within stood corrals of thorn branches, and at the very center was the *nabo*, a ring of thorns where a small fire constantly burned. When the *gob* is moved, as it is three to five times a year, the first fire is lit in the *nabo*. From it, each woman collects embers to kindle the cooking fire in her hut.

"The *nabo* is the center of our lives," Galyago explained.

(Above and right)
Rendille women
assembling hut,
gob Saale.

"Every night all of us elders gather here to talk about the health of the camels, when to move the *gob*, everything. You see, for us, life is discussions."

As we strolled around, I was struck by the feeling of community within the circle of huts. A group of elders discussed what might be done about a lion that had killed one of their camels the previous night. Children played together while women sat in shade cast by their huts, stringing beads for jewelry, weaving mats from wild sisal gathered in the distant mountains.

"You see this *gob*. This is our way," Galyago said. "Why should I or any Rendille want the town? No, no. Oh, sometimes we go to get things from the *duka*, but we don't like to stay there. What would we do in that place? There is nothing. In the *gob*, we have our families and camels. The clan is here with us.

"In the rainy season, all the people and all the camels, sheep, and goats are here in the *gob*. But when it gets dry like now, there is not enough food for the animals to eat—we only keep a few for milk to feed us old people and children. The warriors take the herds far away in the bush.

"There are no houses there; they sleep on the ground, and they are always moving [up to 25 miles a day], searching for food, digging water from the *luggas*, protecting the animals from lions. The boys go with them when they are about six, like my eldest son who is there now. They help the warriors look after the herds, and they learn how to live in the bush, so when it is their turn to be warriors, they will know what to do. The clan depends on them because camels are everything to us. And the bush is not like the *gob*. You have to be strong

15

16   *Rendille woman and child near Korr.*

and clever there. It is a dangerous place."

We were interrupted by a pair of warriors who came running to the *gob*, looking for Galyago. Two boys tending the herds with them about 20 miles away had gotten into a fight. One had put his spear through the other's foot.

We rushed to the car and drove as fast as we could through the thorn scrub and sand *lugga*s until we found the boy, who was about eight, in the shade of an acacia. The spear had gone right through his foot, luckily pushing aside, rather than piercing, veins and bones along the way. We had no anesthetic, but the boy was surprisingly calm. The Rendille prize stoic tolerance of pain. When this boy is circumcised upon initiation into warriorhood at about age 14, his standing in his age set will be largely determined by his ability to show no signs of discomfort. He grimaced only slightly as Liz cleaned the wound and then stitched the top together, leaving the bottom open to drain.

Rendille child, gob Saale.

It was dusk when we arrived back at the *gob*. The full moon, rising in concert with the setting sun, lay squashed and orange on the horizon, silhouetting the herds of milk camels being driven back to the safety of their corrals. We carried the boy into his mother's hut, trying to reassure her that he would be all right. Galyago escorted us to our campsite, then headed for the *nabo* to discuss the other boy's punishment. Liz and I crawled into the tent, exhausted.

Near midnight, I was awakened by a low voice. It was Galyago. He had brought us some camel's milk.

*Rendille woman
near Korr.*

On our last day at the *gob*, Galyago took Liz and me to meet with Sono, the "elder in charge of talking." He was nearly 100 years old, he reckoned, though there was no way of knowing his exact age. Satim said he was the oldest of all the Rendille.

"You see," Sono told us, "all I can do anymore is talk. But we Rendille say a man is wise if he can confuse the others and get them to do what he wants. We are impressed by men who can speak well. I admire this thing you can do, this writing. You put words in that book and go there later to get them back. That is very good."

Sono was born about the time Europeans first drew boundaries on their map of Africa, arbitrarily carving the continent up into the nations that exist today. I was curious to know if life had changed much since those definitions were imposed.

"Our customs have not changed," he said. "The life nowadays is better because it is more peaceful. Before we fought with the Boran and the Turkana. We stole animals and killed each other. The British stopped the fighting when they came to this area, and now there is not so much.

"Before we depended on our animals alone. Now we can buy food if we have to. But the rest is as it was, things like blessing the animals and bringing up children. Some Rendille clans have mixed up with the Samburu and taken their customs. They even forget their own language. But here we still follow the pure ways of Rendille."

A quality of spirituality seemed to pervade those ways. Once as I was driving several women to the distant wells, one of them called out for us to stop. Satim explained that her father had died near the spot about 20 years earlier, and that the woman could not pass without pausing to greet his spirit. We all piled out of the car and took turns pouring milk into the small holes she scooped in the earth while she prayed.

But the Rendille also seemed remarkably pragmatic. I asked Sono about religion. "Sometimes strangers come into the *gob* with ideas from outside," he told me. "They call themselves Moslem; others say they are Christian. They talk a lot but do not make sense. They say they know what happens when you die. How can they know those things? 'All right,' we say to them, 'you bring someone who has been to your heaven or your hell. Then maybe we will listen to you.'

"Of course there are spirits, and they can help us," Sono explained. "If a camel is lost, I can pray to the spirit of my father to help me get it back. When a person dies, we know that he is dead, and we know what happens to his body because we take it out of the *gob* and put it in the sand. But how can anybody know where the spirit goes if they can't see it come out? Nobody can know beyond death. I will find out when I die, and that is enough."

I told Sono that we were leaving for the south the next day, "going to Kenya," as Galyago had put it. Sono said he hoped our stay had been enjoyable and that we would not forget the Rendille after we had gone. I assured him that would be impossible.

"May God give you strength of health and wealth," Sono said, blessing us.

"May God make your name be as high as a mountain.

"May God make you a leader of all those with five fingers.

"May God give you a lot of years to stay in this world like me now."

Sono, gob Saale.

19

(Above and left) Ariaal Rendille watching videotape of wedding, near Laisamis. 21

El Molo herdsmen driving cattle near Loyangalani.

(Right) El Molo man and child near Loyangalani.

22 *(Pages 24-25) Samburu herdsman near South Horr.*

26   *White-headed vulture perched on duom palm, Samburu Game Reserve.*

Impala with red-billed oxpecker. 27

Gerenuk, Samburu Game Reserve.

28   *(Right) African elephants, Ewaso Ng'iro River, Samburu Game Reserve.*

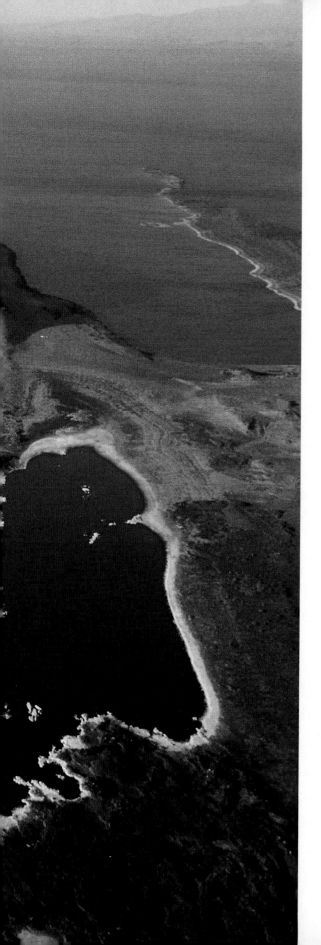

(Above and pages 32-33) Magado Crater.

(Left) Volcanic crater with lava flow, south end of Lake Turkana.   31

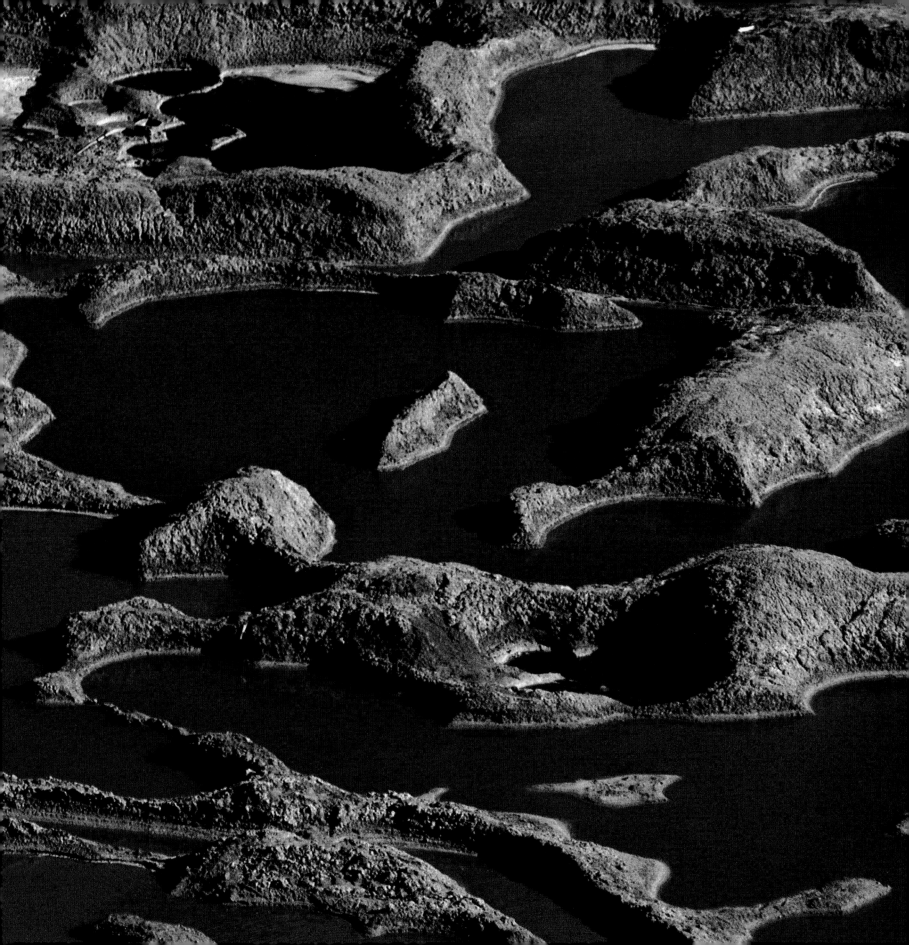

THE CENTRAL HIGHLANDS

Rain thundered on the tin roof of the clay-and-wattle house and pounded the earthen yard, sending sprays of muddy water in through the doorway. The roof, fashioned 10 years earlier from flattened kerosene tins, leaked in several spots where it had rusted through, making little pools in the dirt floor. The door was slightly ajar, but vented only a fraction of the smoke from the cooking fire around which we huddled. Nights are cold at 6,000 feet, even so near the equator.

Susan sat by the fire, stoking it with thin branches, while Njoroge, her husband, played with Nganga, their two-year-old son. Julius, seven, leaned against his father on the low bench, fast asleep. The two girls, Njeri, five, and Beati, Nganga's twin, watched their mother tilt a pot toward the dim light of the kerosene lantern to see if the vegetables were done. They weren't, and Susan sent Njeri to fetch some water out of a basin that caught runoff from a piece of gutter over the doorway.

When the food was ready, Njeri went back into the rain to get dishes from atop the chicken coop where they were stored above the splashing mud. Susan spooned mounds of potatoes and cabbage into plastic bowls and handed them around.

"You have to eat a lot when it is cold like this," she said.

I had found Njoroge and his family a few days earlier while traveling through the area with officials from the Central Bureau of Statistics. I was looking for a representative Kenyan family to profile for a *National Geographic* story about world population, but it was not easy to find one that fit the parameters the magazine had given me and was willing to let me stay with them for two weeks. Many people were suspicious; they couldn't believe I wanted to spend that much time on a small farm just to document their daily lives. Njoroge and Susan

*Susan carrying
napier grass for
cattle fodder.*

didn't really understand what I was doing either, but they welcomed me nonetheless and quickly made me feel like one of the family.

Njoroge's farm is perched on one of the ridges that pour off the Aberdare Mountains in Central Province. It is a fertile, crowded land. Roads, usually dirt, along the ridges are lined with houses like Njoroge's, though some are larger and made of stone and tile. The farms are thin bands. Food crops—maize, beans, potatoes, sweet potatoes, cassava, bananas, and a cabbage called *sukuma weeki* (the name means "to push through the week")—grow in patches around the houses and at the valley floors. The slopes between are covered with cash crops: coffee in Njoroge's zone, tea higher up. Njoroge's farm is about 10 yards wide and 200 yards long.

Both Susan, 25, and Njoroge, 28, had been educated through seventh grade. "I could not go after that because of trouble with money," Njoroge said. Though taught in English, they have rarely used it since leaving school; Kikuyu and Swahili meet their daily needs. When I first arrived, both their English and my Swahili were rusty. By the time I left, we were getting along quite well with a mixture of the two.

"You see how we are living now," Njoroge told me after finishing his meal. "The rain comes in the house. But I can't get money for a new roof.

"We can't survive with just this farm. We can't grow enough food or even coffee to pay for everything. My father's farm was three acres, and that was okay. But he had eleven children—everyone had big families in those days—and six of us were boys. Now, for us Kikuyu, every son has to get a part of his father's land. So I have only half an acre. It's too little even for a small family like us."

Njoroge's problems are typical of those facing Kikuyu and other farming peoples. Comprising more than 20 percent of the population, the Kikuyu are Kenya's largest ethnic group and have had profound influence on the politics and economy of the country. Because they lived in the area of heaviest European settlement, they felt the influence of the British earlier and more intensely than other groups. And they were adaptable, taking easily to the new mission schools and to jobs in colonial offices and on settlers' farms. Later, Kikuyus were in the vanguard of the independence movement and led the country under President Jomo Kenyatta for the first 15 years of nationhood.

Kikuyus benefited from their influential role; central Kenya is more developed than any other place I have seen in 17 years of African travel. Roads lace the countryside. Schools, health facilities, agricultural extension services, and markets are plentiful.

But the Kikuyu, like other groups in the rapidly developing parts of Kenya, are victims of their own success: customs and attitudes are harder to change than infrastructure. In the years after independence, as life expectancy increased and infant mortality decreased, the population exploded. For many years, Kenyan officials ignored the problem, and the annual growth rate climbed to 4.2 percent, the world's highest. Now, almost every speech by government leaders includes a lecture on family planning. Birth control information and devices are readily available in the more developed, more critical areas. The growth rate in the central highlands, once the nation's highest, has begun to drop. Nonetheless, 53 percent of the population is under 14, and the number of Kenyans will double before Nganga and Beati are 20 years old.

Six half-acre plots owned by Njoroge and his five brothers.

37

Eighty-five percent of Kenyans are cultivators, but only about 20 percent of the country is good, arable land; already population pressure has pushed farmers into marginal land, with predictably marginal results. Small holdings have been divided among the many sons of large families, leaving people like Njoroge unable to produce either enough food or enough cash crops to survive in the modern economy. Most families have one wage earner who often must work and live far from his family. The shantytowns around Nairobi swell with people from the countryside, but jobs are scarce.

"When I finished standard seven, I went to Nairobi to look for a job as a laborer," Njoroge told me early the next morning as we stood in the small yard, looking east to the jagged, snow-capped peaks of Mount Kenya. "I stayed six months. One day I had to carry cement from the ground to the fifth floor. I started at eight in the morning and carried cement until three in the night. For this I was paid 18 shillings [about $2 at the time]. When we finished, I told the other men, 'I can't do this work one more day.' I took my money and came home.

"I will never go back to Nairobi. The life there is bad, and what good does it do? My brother has worked there for 17 years, but look at him. He has to pay for a room in Nairobi, food, and transport from there to here. He has a small house made of mud and one cow, just like me. It has not helped him to be there."

To supplement his farm income, Njoroge learned stone masonry and works in the area when he can find jobs, about half the time, making 80 shillings ($4.75) a day. Susan works as casual labor during planting and harvest on bigger farms for 20 shillings when her chores at home permit.

Julius peering through window. (Left) Njeri having her hair done by her cousin.

Njeri washing Beati's face.

At 6:45, Njoroge ran to catch the *matatu* (group taxi) climbing up the slippery slope behind the house. To his job site, the fare was four shillings, the round trip a tenth of his wage.

Susan milked the cow in the open shed just outside the fence that enclosed the yard, then poured most of the pint and a half she got into the children's tea. Njeri washed the twins' faces and hands in rainwater, handed them each a cup of tea and a lump of *ugali*, and sat down to eat her own.

Julius opened the shed and drove the cow off to graze along the road; he tended it all day while school was on vacation. Susan walked down to a maize and potato patch below the house, eyed it for a while, then called to Njeri to bring her the *panga* (machete). Njeri fetched it from the house and handed it to Nganga, who set off with the *panga*, almost as big as he, for the field. Susan bent over, legs straight, plunging the *panga* into the red earth with one hand, uprooting weeds with the other.

By 10:00, the sun was fiercely hot. Susan went farther down the slope where she cut napier grass from the terrace edges beneath the coffee trees and lugged it up the steep path to the cow's trough. She then pulled a basin to the edge of the yard, washed the children's clothes, and hung them to dry. She stoked the fire to make lunch, tea and *ugali* with cabbage. At 2:00, Susan went off to work.

I stayed on the farm with the children. Njeri looked after the twins, who ran between their house and their aunt's next door. There was always a casual flow between the two houses of this extended family, and items—a radio, a pair of knitting needles, cooking pots—moved back and forth as they were needed. But I was struck with the difference between this existence and the open, more communal way of the Rendille

Susan shopping, Githumu.   41

Njeri and friend jumping rope.

in the north. Farmers live in huts on
small pieces of private property. The
toil required to tend the land leaves
little time for socializing beyond the
family, and there is no need for con-
sensus in reaching decisions. While
they are part of a much more extensive
and intricate network than the nomadic Rendille, their world of daily
interaction is much smaller.

During the second week of my stay
on the farm, it was classic rainy season
weather: cold, misty mornings followed by hot middays that caused
clouds to bank up against the
Aberdares, then burst in afternoon
downpours often lasting all night.

Njoroge's construction job was
suspended, and he took advantage of

Njoroge spraying coffee trees.

being home to work in the coffee. As with most Kenyan
agriculturalists, Kikuyu men are largely responsible for the
cash crops, women for the food. "You know, the woman
cannot finish the work of the coffee, the terracing and
spraying," Njoroge said, mixing a batch of copper sulfate.
"That is why it is not good to work in Nairobi, but to stay
here. When I am not working, I can tend my trees."

He sprayed each one carefully with a hand-pumped
backpack rig that leaked and spewed the chemical into his
face. Like his fertilizer, the chemicals are obtained from the
coffee factory on credit against his crop. The year before, he
harvested 500 kilos of coffee beans from 120 trees; 130 more

had been planted but were not yet mature. He earned 5.33 shillings a kilo (about 14 cents a pound), and his previous year's crop netted him about $120.00.

"We have to pay school building fees for Julius and Njeri, though the one for nursery school is small," Njoroge told me as he rested on one of the terraces. "And we have to buy school uniforms, exercise books, and pencils. The school is taking almost all the money we get from coffee. That is why I must work. If it is so expensive now, how will we manage when the twins are older, when all four are in school?

"But education is the most important thing. I can't divide this farm between Julius and Nganga. It is too small, they could not live. They will have to go buy land in another place, but how will they get the money? They will have to find jobs. I don't have any relations who are big men who can get jobs for my sons. So they have to get education. Otherwise they have no chance."

"That is the reason we stopped our family with these children," said Susan, who had carried a pail of water down from the house to mix more spray. "If we have more, how could we send them to school? How could we feed them? It is not just the youngest—all of them would suffer."

I asked Njoroge what he would do if he had a lot of money.

Julius in class, Gitare Primary School near Githumu.
(Left) Flag raising at the school.

"I would buy land," he replied without hesitating. "If I had two acres, I would be very, very happy. I do not want very much; two acres can give me enough. I like working on my land."

Susan and Njoroge, like most Kenyans, are completely caught up in the modern cash economy. Their aspirations are for the better life as defined by the Western values their developing country has adopted. To the visitor's eye, little of Kikuyu tradition remains. In the two weeks I spent in Central Province, I saw only one very ancient woman with the ear loops and hide dress that once characterized the Kikuyu.

Nairobi is perhaps the most dramatic evidence of this rapid transformation. Communications and services are good; the streets throng with briefcase-toting Kenyan and foreign businessmen. Nairobi is virtually indistinguishable from a city of similar size anywhere in the world. It just happens to include within its city limits a national park where lions, cheetahs, giraffes, rhinoceroses, and other beasts roam.

Ngenye Kariuki, the president of the Nairobi Stock Exchange, met with me in his office overlooking the city center. The jacket of his three-piece suit was thrown over a chair, and he was sorting through files he needed to take on his trip. He was leaving for New York the next day to attend meetings on Wall Street. The weekend before, he had visited his parents on their farm not far from Njoroge's.

"You know, just this weekend I was thinking how things have changed here, how astonishingly fast it's been," he said. "My grandfather did not know what money was. He lived on his farm, trading maize and beans for what he needed. Now I sit in an office and worry about how the rate for Japanese yen will affect our stock index."

Wedding party, Limuru.

(Left) Sikh bride with friends, Nairobi.   49

Luo woman carrying fish near Kisumu.

50 *(Right) Lake Victoria.*

52   *Luo man with his two wives.*

Luo baby near Kisumu. 53

Tea plucker, Kericho.

(Right) Tea estate, Sotik.

54 (Pages 56-57) Wheat farms, Timau.

58   *Mount Kenya.*

Polo players, Timau. 59

60   *Reticulated giraffe, Meru National Park.*

62   *Cape buffalo, Nairobi National Park.*

Male ostrich on nest, Nairobi National Park.   63

64   *Black rhinoceros, Aberdare National Park.*

Park ranger guarding white rhinoceroses, Meru National Park.

(Pages 66-67) White rhinoceroses, Solio.

THE SWAHILI COAST

The six-seater plane took off from Mombasa airport, banked over the town, and headed north along the coast. The pilot checked his bearings on the map and asked the sweating businessman who had squeezed into the copilot's seat to mind the rudder pedals on the floor. Two elderly women draped head to foot in black *buibuis* perched in the middle seats, alternately staring out the window at the receding ground and burying their heads in the seat backs in front of them. Next to me sat a young American wearing baggy shorts and an oversized T-shirt that read *Hakuna Matata* (No Problem).

We followed the paved coast road to Malindi, flying over factories, huge sisal and cashew estates, and the tourist hotels that line the shore. After Malindi, the road, now dirt, meanders through scattered farms and past thatched huts that lie inland from miles of pristine beaches and palm-studded dunes.

It was not a pleasant flight; we flew below heavy clouds, through rain and violent winds. The women prayed. Every so often, one of them turned to look at me for reassurance, as if I had anything to do with our fate. I smiled at her. She grinned back stiffly, said in Arabic, "God is great," and buried her head once more.

About an hour after takeoff, we descended over the dense green mangrove swamps that fringe the Lamu archipelago. The town of Lamu, a cluster of white buildings on one of the islands, slopes up from a sea wall off which lateen-sailed boats were moored. We landed at the airstrip on Manda Island which protects Lamu and its harbor from the open sea.

Though only 150 miles from Mombasa, albeit over a very rough and sometimes impassable road, Lamu's ties with the

70   *Lamu waterfront.*

rest of Kenya have always been tenuous; her genesis was in maritime trade, her influences seaborne. Sheltered water made Lamu a convenient port for Arabian dhows plying the East African coast, a trade that began in pre-Islamic times. Northeast monsoons from November to April carried the dhows south from Arabia to Zanzibar and beyond, bringing silks, spices, Chinese porcelain, and carpets. They returned from June to October on the southwest monsoon, laden with ivory, rhinoceros horns, mangrove poles, cowrie and tortoise shells, and slaves from the African interior. The trade spawned coastal settlements where merchants and mariners, bringing their cultures and Islamic religion, married Bantu women of the coast. Powerful city-states arose, supported by inland plantations of grain and fruit. A new people, culture, and language were born: Swahili.

Lamu flourished from the 17th to 19th centuries, and is one of the few Swahili city-states to have survived somewhat intact. Most succumbed to economic decline and reverted to villages or fell entirely to ruin. Others, like Mombasa and Malindi, became part of modern Kenya's mainstream; their indigenous cultures have been largely overwhelmed. Lamu, a district capital of about 12,000 people, is isolated on the northern coast. It feels the pressure of modernity from upcountry government officials and the foreigners who seek its beaches, but has managed so far to maintain its traditions.

I arrived in Lamu just before the end of Ramadan, the Moslem month of dawn-to-dusk fasting. At midday, when the

Ithna-Asheri Mosque, Lamu.

shops were shuttered and the town still, amplified prayers from several of the 23 mosques echoed down narrow alleys enclosed by high, windowless walls. Only the heavy, elaborately carved doors hint at the artistry created in these homes during Lamu's heyday: decorative plasterwork, ornate wall niches, carved furniture, and sophisticated bathrooms. Two-foot-thick walls of coral blocks keep out heat and noise; central courtyards provide light. Just as the Rendille's circular village and the Kikuyu farmer Njoroge's hut reflect their inhabitants' culture, the architecture of Lamu reveals the town's history as a mercantile Moslem society that encourages privacy and discourages ostentation.

Most alleys run downhill, funneling rain and wash water to the sea. About five feet wide, they get little sun and act as cooling wind tunnels. Only Main Street, created by landfill in 1830, runs the length of the town parallel to the shore.

I walked down Main Street, shouldering through the afternoon crowds, squeezing past pushcarts. (Bicycles and cars are banned from the island, except for the district commissioner's Land Rover, which is confined to the wide seaside promenade.) Groups of men, sandals off, legs tucked beneath them, sat on cement benches set into the walls. I sat down next to an elderly man and was surprised when he greeted me in Arabic, "*Salaam Alaikum*." But then he switched to Swahili, a Bantu language very much modified by Arabic and, recently, by English. Following caravans that penetrated into the interior, Swahili became the trade language as far west as the Congo Basin, though its purity decreases with distance from the coast.

People followed those trade routes, too, and the reach of Lamu's commerce can be seen in the diversity of its popula-

72 *Riyadha Mosque, Lamu.*

Bajun woman, Matandoni,
Lamu Island.

tion. Swahili is a cultural definition, not one of blood. Some of the men and women walking along the street looked as if they had just arrived from the deserts of Yemen, others from the rain forests of Zaire.

"Kenya is many kinds of people," the man said. "It causes us some problems, but it also makes Kenya work." We sat in silence for a while, watching the passersby. One was a European or American woman, young and scruffy, wearing a sleeveless shirt that revealed more than is considered proper in Lamu. Her head was shaved, her countenance grim. "She must come from a country with a lot of problems," the old man said, shaking his head.

As dusk approached, more people drifted into the street. Vendors set out pastries and skewers of roasting meat. One slashed the tops off green coconuts to reveal the sweet milk and translucent flesh. Shortly after 6:00, the mullah's call announced the end of the daily fast, and the noise level dropped. Everybody was eating for the first time since before dawn.

I noticed children scampering to rooftops, looking westward in hopes of sighting the new moon—its appearance signals the end of Ramadan. But the sky was too bright, the moon too close to the setting sun. The fast would go on another day.

The next morning, I walked to the southern part of town, an area of mud-and-thatch houses. On an earlier visit in 1985, I had seen mangrove poles stacked high along the sea wall and laborers moving back and forth, loading lighters that ferried the poles to freighters anchored in the strait. In 1988, the waterfront was quiet.

Mangrove grows profusely in the archipelago and for centuries was a major export. Shipped to treeless Arabia as

Stick dance during wedding ceremony, Lamu.   75

76   *Workers loading mangrove poles before export ban, Lamu.*

a building material, the nine-foot lengths even dictated elements of Arabian architecture. When oil wealth enabled Arabians to afford costlier materials, mangrove remained much in demand as scaffolding. But in the early 1980s, as freighters replaced dhows, the character of the ancient trade changed.

"It is four years since the dhows stopped and the engines started coming," a merchant told me in 1985. "The ships take too much mangrove to Arabia, and the price has dropped.

"The dhows carried coconuts, tamarinds, and mangoes. But the ships take only mangrove, so we have lost our market for other things. And the dhows brought dates, spices, raisins, carpets, and clothes. These big ships bring nothing to Lamu."

The monsoons dictated the pace of commerce for dhows. Freighters, able to come and go as they please, carried away so much mangrove that the swamps were overharvested and the government has been forced to ban its export. Owners of the mangrove plots have lost their income, merchants have lost their trade, and countless laborers who cut the poles have lost their jobs.

"Lamu is dead," one young entrepreneur told me. "We can't export mangrove, so the economy suffers. The tourists with money don't come. They stay in Malindi or Mombasa. We only get the ones who stay in cheap rooms and lie on the beach all day, playing cards and reading paperbacks."

Tourism is one of the few alternatives available to Lamu's economy, but it is a mixed blessing. The tourists seem to

Swahili men sitting along Main Street, Lamu.

Children buying kebabs
during Idd al Fitr, Lamu.

want little more than sun and sand from Lamu and appear unaware of the profound effect they have on the island's culture. Many walk through town clad only in their bathing suits. The seaward side of the island, where they spend their days, boasts eight miles of gloriously isolated beach, but some tourists go only about 50 yards from the village of Shela before stripping to sunbathe nude within sight of the bewildered and offended islanders.

"If you ask the beach boys, they would like more of these travelers to come because it is an opportunity to make money," one older Swahili man told me. "They have developed a gigolo mentality. But many of us are worried about cultural pollution, about the effects foreigners are having, especially on our young people. Look at what has happened to Malindi. It is just a tourist town now; it is not Swahili anymore.

"Sometimes we ask them to put on a shirt if they are walking through town or in a restaurant, but they get angry. One even yelled at me, 'Hey, this is a beach town.' What can we do? We need tourists, but we are afraid of them."

Foreigners and their ways are a topic of constant conversation and concern among the town elders. They cherish their traditions and identity and, being well-mannered, are troubled by the seeming insensitivity of their visitors. A sign in the Lamu Museum reads in part, "We ask that you respect our culture by dressing and behaving in a proper manner…. Please tread gently here, our children are watching you."

The last evening of Ramadan, I stood on the balcony of my room, looking west like the children gathered on surrounding rooftops. We waited. Then the sky grew just dark enough to show, through parting rainy season clouds, a hair-thin sliver of moon. The children clapped and yelled. The fast was over; tomorrow was Idd al Fitr.

Everybody was out early the next morning, strolling the streets, greeting each other with elaborate protocol. The men wore brilliant white robes and delicately embroidered caps called *kofia*s. Beneath their *buibui*s, the women revealed glimpses of new dresses and hands and feet freshly decorated with henna designs. All the children had bright new clothes. The girls wore dresses and socks trimmed with lace.

Adults visited friends and relatives, sharing tea and sweet cakes. Children went from house to house, where they were given coins to spend at the food kiosks in the street.

"Everyone is in a good mood," a friend told me. "The alms were good this year." By tradition, individuals give 2.5 percent of their money, and merchants 2.5 percent of their stock to the needy. Thus wealth is redistributed, and the bonds of the community reinforced.

That afternoon, a fair was held at the primary school. I found it by following the streams of women and children who poured toward the distorted music blaring from enormous speakers; Madonna's "Like a Virgin" could be heard all over town. The schoolyard was crowded with kiosks selling flavored ices and green mangoes sprinkled with spice. Classrooms had been transformed into throbbing discos. A merry-go-round powered by teenagers lured flocks of young

Painting henna designs for Idd al Fitr, Lamu.

79

Lamu street scene.

children. Older children and their mothers giggled and screamed in the buckets of a hand-cranked Ferris wheel.

The women especially seemed to enjoy the fair. In Lamu, as in other traditional Islamic towns, women lead sheltered lives—some rarely leave their homes. Contact with young men, courtship, and marriage are overseen by their elders and prescribed by custom. While young men now wear mostly Western clothes, women are rarely seen in public except when wrapped in *buibui*s. The effect of foreign attitudes and behavior on women's traditional role is one of the townspeople's concerns. Many of the men and women with whom I talked are afraid that change will happen too quickly and disrupt not only institutions, but people's relationships with each other.

In the evening, most of the mothers and children went home. Groups of young women remained, and young men, having changed into natty Western dress, arrived. One of them came up to me. He wore jeans, a flowery shirt, sunglasses, and a cap from a ship of the U.S. Navy's 7th Fleet which makes calls at Mombasa.

"Hi, guy," he grinned. "Where you from?"

I shook his hand, told him I was American.

"Yeah? That's really cool, man. I hung out with American sailors in Mombasa. They're really wild. We had a good time."

The young man leaned against a palm tree and pulled at his cigarette. His eyes followed a group of veiled young women who walked past.

"How do you like these Lamu chicks?" he asked. "These chicks are really all right, huh, man?"

Swahili women at the fair, Lamu.

(Pages 82-83) Sisal estate north of Mombasa. 81

Sisal fibers drying.

84   *(Right) Worker cutting sisal.*

Masai trinket sellers and tourists, Diani Beach.

(Right) Tourists, Diani Beach.

87

88   *(Above and right) Dhows, old Mombasa harbor.*

The text on the sign reads:

ALI'S CURIO MARKET

DEALERS IN:
ANTIQUES
SILVER JEWELLERY
AFRICAN MASKS
LAMU COFFEE POT
ARAB CHEST
BATIKS
ETHIOPIAN CARPETS
WOOD CARVINGS
SEMI PRECIOUS GEMS
TIGER'S EYE
CORAL MALACHITE
JADE ETC. ETC.

90   (*Above and right*) *Mombasa street scenes.*

Swahili woman and tailor, Mombasa.

(Left) Women shopping for kangas.   93

THE MASAI MARA

One August morning, the wind blows across the plains of the Masai Mara, Kenya's most popular game reserve, bending the yellow grass where wildebeests and zebras haven't grazed it to a stubble. Topi stand guard on weathered, gray termite mounds. Crowned plovers fly up shrieking, trying to distract a jackal that is foraging too close to their nest in the grass.

From beyond the horizon, thousands of wildebeests approach in long lines, beating paths to the Mara River. Crocodiles slip into the water. Vultures circle overhead or perch in trees, waiting for what they know is about to happen. I hide in the bush along the river, waiting, too.

The herds converge on the bank, funneled by the riverine forest into a great mass of bodies. Those in the lead stop, staring at the water ten feet below. They're nervous in the thick vegetation—good cover for predators.

More and more wildebeests stream in from the plains until the building pressure forces the lead animals to plunge into the water. As if a signal has been given, the whole herd rushes, pushing toward the bank, leaping and crashing into the river which disappears beneath a snorting, struggling throng. Thousands of hooves grind the steep opposite bank into a slippery paste, leaving no firm hold. Desperate animals clamber over each other, or slip and slide back into the water. Exhausted, many are carried away by the current and drown.

The river is clogged with carcasses. Crocs tear at them under the surface; vultures peck at the flesh. The toll is astounding. Yet the herd survives, even prospers. By next year, its numbers will likely have grown.

That morning, I was witnessing one of Africa's most awe-inspiring spectacles, the wildebeest migration. About

Wildebeests crossing Mara River, Masai Mara Reserve.

1.5 million of these large antelopes leave Tanzania's Serengeti National Park each year and trek into the Mara, the northern end of the Serengeti ecosystem. The herds spend several weeks there devouring the grass until rains in the south lure them back to Tanzania.

Bounded by the Loita Hills in the east and by the great wall of the Esoit Oloololo Escarpment in the west, the Mara's undulating savannah is laced with seasonal streambeds, dotted with acacia woodlands and dense thickets. Not only wildebeests flourish here: the Mara is home to 92 species of mammals, including elephants, rhinoceroses, giraffes, and lions, and 450 species of birds, 53 of which are birds of prey.

To Europeans and Americans, Kenya's wildlife has always been a great attraction. A turn-of-the-century British poster, showing a train besieged by wild beasts, proclaimed, "The Highlands of British East Africa as a Winter Home for Aristocrats Has Become A Fashion. Sportsmen in search of Big Game make it a Hobby. Students of Natural History revel in this Field of Nature's Own Making." No other place in the world could match East Africa's combination of ideal climate, magnificent scenery, and plentiful big game. Natural history, though, ran a poor second to hunting in those days; most early accounts of animal behavior ended abruptly when the subject came within rifle range.

By the 1970s, Kenya's exploding population was restricting wildlife habitats, and poaching had caused catastrophic declines in many species. Under pressure from international conservation groups and seeking to preserve its tourist industry, the Kenyan government banned all hunting in 1977. The age of the big game safari, as Theodore Roosevelt and Ernest Hemingway lived it, was over.

Lake Magadi, Great Rift Valley. 97

White rhinoceroses
(two of the six killed
by poachers in 1988),
Meru National Park.

Despite the hunting ban, the threat of extinction still hangs over many species. Poaching continued unabated, fueled by sky-high profits on the black-market sale of rhino horns and elephant tusks. When I first visited the Mara in 1972, black rhinos were plentiful; I found them easily every day. Now one has to be extremely lucky to see rhinos in the reserve. The losses throughout Kenya are staggering. In the early 1970s, the black rhinoceros population was around 20,000. By mid-1988, only about 350 survived—a drop of 98 percent in 15 years.

Kenya's elephant statistics are just as depressing: 130,570 in 1973, about 16,000 today. Big-tusked elephants, the poachers' favorite targets, are extremely rare nowadays, but the slaughter has been indiscriminate. On several occasions, I've seen entire herds of elephants which had been mowed down by machine guns. Many of the dead were youngsters, their faces mutilated to remove what can only have been very tiny tusks. I've also seen the unmistakable sadness elephants display when they come upon the butchered bodies of their fellows, watched the herd stand silently over the dead, touching them gently with their trunks.

A herd of elephants can wipe out a farmer's entire maize crop in one night, and many Kenyans, including some game rangers, are understandably tempted by the prospect of getting the equivalent of several years' wages for a single rhino horn. But the poaching epidemic was not caused by individuals seeking to protect their farms or feed their children. Poaching was big business, often run in collusion with government officials. While underpaid park rangers were equipped with old rifles, never had enough ammunition, and were often without fuel for their dilapidated vehicles, the poaching gangs had automatic weapons and carried off their loot in new trucks. They used chain saws to gouge the tusks from elephants' faces. The poachers grew increasingly bold: In late 1988, members of one gang attacked the headquarters of Meru National Park, keeping the rangers pinned down while their companions slaughtered six white rhinoceroses fenced in a nearby corral for protection.

The situation was becoming intolerable; elephant and rhino populations in Kenya and many other African states were nearing extinction. In the late 1980s, Kenyan elephants were being slaughtered at the rate of 150 a week. Scientists estimated that if poaching continued unabated, the continent's elephants, some 1.5 million in 1979, might be extinct by the turn of the century. Most countries have been unable to control poaching; the vast sums of money involved easily corrupt government officials, often right up to the top.

In 1989, the world community decided to attack poaching at the other end, the market. African elephants were placed on the endangered species list (rhinos had long been there), and all international trade in ivory was banned. Pressure was put on African governments to clean up their acts. Large sums of money and equipment were donated to park systems and to organizations policing wildlife traffic.

African elephant, Amboseli National Park.

It worked. As western and oriental markets for ivory dried up, poaching died down. Today, there is very little illegal killing of wildlife in Kenya.

For most African countries, such as Kenya, the ban was the only answer—they simply couldn't, or wouldn't, control the gangs that roamed inside their borders. A few countries, such as Zimbabwe and Botswana, feel they are being unfairly penalized. During the 1970s and 1980s, while elephants and rhinos were being decimated on most of the continent, these countries ran their parks with determination and care. Animal populations flourished. Poaching was so minimal that culling became necessary; burgeoning elephant populations threatened permanent damage to the vegetation in the limited areas set aside for them. Money from the sale of culled ivory was used for park management. The ivory ban robbed these countries of much-needed revenue. Why, they ask, should they be penalized for having run their parks efficiently all these years? Why should their parks suffer because others have been lax and corrupt?

All African countries face severe economic problems, and park management is never a high priority. Hopefully, revenue from tourism can tide the parks over until the time when the world can sustain a small, legal ivory market and countries such as Kenya can run their parks well enough to preclude poaching. There are positive signs already; Kenya's rangers are better paid and equipped than they once were and, more importantly, there seems to be an official will to preserve the country's unique and profitable heritage.

Kenya's wildlife, like that of many African countries, is under pressure not just from poaching. A severe land shortage makes the parks' very existences rather precarious. In a

(Above and left)
Cheetahs and tourists,
Masai Mara Reserve.

101

*Impalas, Amboseli
National Park.*

country where the human population will double in 17 years, Kenya's 13,000 square miles—5.8 percent of its area—of parks and reserves often seem a luxury the people can't afford. Much of this land could be used for agriculture; the Mara's rolling plains would be perfect for wheat. Kenyans like Njoroge and Susan, forced to eke out meager livings on tiny plots in the crowded central highlands, covetously eye the parks. In 1987, tourism surpassed coffee and tea to become Kenya's top source of foreign exchange. If this money is used wisely to develop the country and benefit the entire population, the parks can be justified. Without this revenue, the government would be hard pressed to refuse Kenyans access to the land. As long as the parks make money, they and the animals they shelter have a chance to survive.

Tourism, though, is not a panacea; the growing numbers of tourists and the infrastructure needed to accommodate them have their own impact. In the parks and reserves, the definition of "wild" becomes blurred. These are not the trackless, unvisited spaces of the north where animals are wary and seldom seen. In the early 1970s, there were only a few lodges and tented camps in the Mara. Today there are a dozen and plans for more. Countless tracks crisscross the plains; minibuses and Land Rovers sometimes seem more numerous than the animals they seek.

The animals have become inured to the traffic. Most will flee upon seeing a person on foot even at a great distance, but vehicles no longer rile them. I've had shade-seeking lions crawl under my car and cheetahs jump up on the hood to look around for prey. Being able to approach so near is, of course, a great advantage for tourists, as well as for scientists studying animal behavior and for professional photographers

like myself. It also makes poaching easier. And unless proper care is taken, the crowds of tourists can be disruptive; officials in one park were worried that cheetahs would starve to death because their hunts were so often disturbed by cars rushing ahead to get a better view.

Tourism is a mixed blessing for the animals, and for the people the tourists seek out too. The Mara exists as a sanctuary today largely because its native people, the Masai, are pastoralists who have always shared land with wildlife instead of killing and displacing it as farmers must. But few Masai are able to live as they once did.

Much has been written about the Masai, and they are probably the most photographed of all African people. Everyone wants to go home with a picture of Masai warriors—tall, elegant, draped in red *shuka*s. They stand, spears in hand, gazing out over the African plains, their earlobes, necks, and wrists decorated with beads, long hair braided and smeared red with ocher. Like the Rendille, they are strongly resistant to change. Unlike the Rendille, who live in arid lands few people visit and no one yet covets, the Masai live on well-watered land close to the rapidly developing parts of Kenya. More aware of and affected by the modern world than the Rendille, less embracing of it than the Kikuyu, the Masai must struggle to forge a culture combining elements of their tradition and the imperatives of the nation.

Many Masai have jobs as rangers, tour guides, drivers, and hotel staff; tourism provides much of the cash the Masai need to find their place in the modern world. It won't be easy.

Masai elder near Suswa.
(Left) Masai warriors.

Kenyan officials, embarrassed by "primitive" dress and nomadic culture, press the Masai to abandon their traditions. Westerners looking for an exotic camera subject want the Masai to remain "noble savages." The Masai feel the squeeze. For centuries, pastoral people like the Masai have dealt with conflict by sticking to their ways and moving on. Now there is nowhere to go.

The Masai have already lost most of their land, first to Europeans, then to other Kenyans. Corrupt leaders, both Masai and others, have exploited the Masai's traditional notion of communal land ownership by dividing the land, claiming the deeds, and selling them off. Holdings around the Mara have been leased to wheat farmers in deals that displace many and profit few. The Masai who own the reserve get only 0.6 percent of the revenues it generates.

"We must come to the bargaining table," one young Masai told me. "But this table was built by others, and we do not know the game they play there. That is why we must go to school, so we can learn these new rules."

In 1985, I went to an *eunoto* ceremony marking the passage of Masai warriors into manhood. For several days and nights around the full moon, over 1,000 warriors and their families gathered at a specially built *manyatta* (village) in the Rift Valley. It was a time of dancing and feasts, of symbolism and ritual. But changes were evident. Some initiates were schoolboys taking time off from classes to attend. Family members who worked in Nairobi and other towns came in their cars, wearing coats and ties. A Kikuyu woman set up a stand to sell beer and soft drinks to the crowd.

One of the chiefs, a wizened man draped in monkey skins, told me it would probably be the last time they held the

Masai woman shaving son's head, eunoto *ceremony.*

Masai warriors and girls dancing, eunoto *ceremony.* 107

ceremony, and I felt a twinge of sadness at the passing of an ancient tradition. But when I asked the old man if he was sad too, he surprised me: "No. It is better for these boys to go to school," he said. "With education, they can get jobs and have money to buy more cows and have knowledge so we don't get fooled."

The August morning in the Mara turns to afternoon. The river is quiet. I drive out onto the plains through gathering herds and park under an acacia to scan my surroundings with binoculars. Thomson's gazelles graze, tails going a mile a minute, slender legs beating like pistons because of the flies. One gives birth, and within minutes the baby is up and running.

My eye falls on a limping zebra, partially concealed amid the herd. Her right foreleg is broken. She probably won't survive the night; lions or hyenas will detect her weakness. A wildebeest calf runs zigzagging across the plains, desperately bleating for its mother. Giraffes stroll along the horizon, their outlines simple as cave paintings.

A cheetah climbs a nearby termite mound. Her small cub crawls between her legs, back pressed to its mother's chest. Beyond them, the grasslands roll out to meet a sky flecked orange and pink. The noises of dusk announce yet more creatures, not seen, stirring to their time. Like a faith, I feel the power of this land to transform our inclinations and perchance weather our depredations. It draws me back year after year to witness life's abundance, its fecundity, its diversity—the complex web of relationships that binds each being to the other and all to the African earth.

Cheetahs, Masai Mara Reserve. (Left) Wildebeest migration.

110 *Hippopotamuses, Mara River, Masai Mara Reserve.*

Crocodile eating zebra, Mara River, Masai Mara Reserve. 111

(Above and left) Cape hunting dogs killing wildebeest, Masai Mara Reserve. 113

114   (*Above, right, and pages 116-117*) *Lions, Masai Mara Reserve.*

Lion eating young Masai giraffe, Masai Mara Reserve.

(Right) Lion with Mount Kilamanjaro in background,

118   Amboseli National Park.

(Above and right) African elephants,

120   Amboseli National Park.

Cape buffaloes at water hole,
Tsavo National Park.
(Left) Tsavo National Park. 123

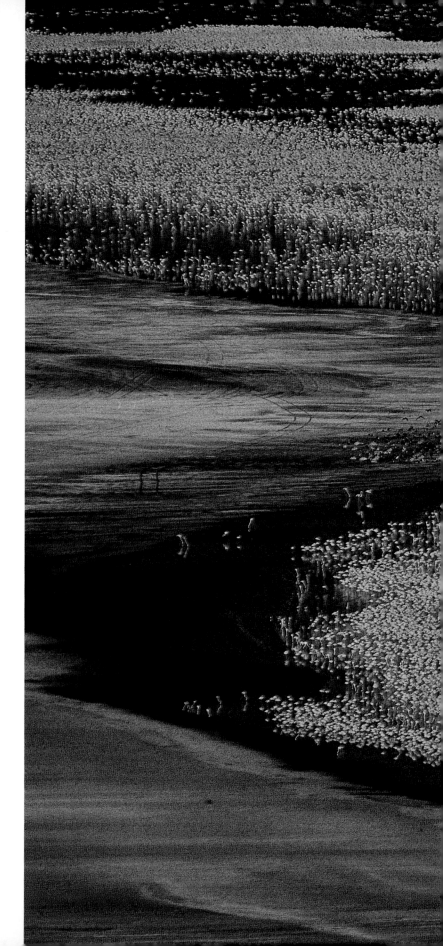

126   (*Above and right*) *Masai manyatta, Great Rift Valley.*

128   *Masai elders resting, eunoto ceremony.*

Masai warriors and girl.   129

130   Eunoto *ceremony*.

Masai warrior blowing kudu horn.   131

Wildebeests, Masai Mara Reserve.

Designed by Gibson Parsons Design
Edited by Elizabeth L.T. Brown
Photography and text by Robert Caputo

Printed and bound in Hong Kong by Everbest Printing Company through Four Colour Imports

98 97 96 95 94 93 92   5 4 3 2 1
Any inquiries should be directed to Elliott & Clark Publishing,
1638 R Street NW, Suite 21, Washington, DC 20009
(202) 387-9805

Library of Congress Cataloging-in-Publication Data
Caputo, Robert.
     Kenya Journal / Robert Caputo.
        p.   cm.
     ISBN 1-880216-03-5
     1. Kenya—Description and travel—1981–   2. Kenya—Pictorial
works.   I.Title.
DT433.527.C37   1992
916.762 ' 044—dc20   91-47150
                                  CIP
                                  AC

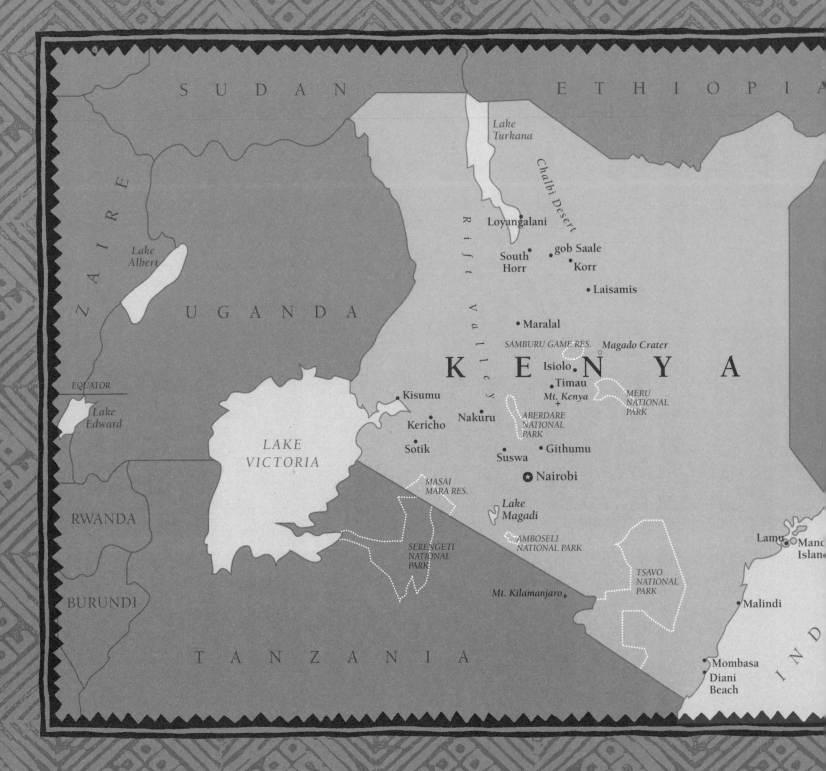

SUDAN

ETHIOPIA

ZAIRE

Lake
Turkana

Chalbi Desert

Lake
Albert

Rift valley

Loyangalani

South
Horr

gob Saale

Korr

UGANDA

Laisamis

Maralal

SAMBURU GAME RES.

Magado Crater

KENYA

Isiolo

EQUATOR

Timau

Kisumu

Mt. Kenya

MERU
NATIONAL
PARK

Lake
Edward

Nakuru

Kericho

ABERDARE
NATIONAL
PARK

RWANDA

Sotik

LAKE
VICTORIA

Suswa

Githumu

Nairobi

BURUNDI

MASAI
MARA RES.

Lake
Magadi

Lamu

Manc
Island

SERENGETI
NATIONAL
PARK

AMBOSELI
NATIONAL PARK

TSAVO
NATIONAL
PARK

Mt. Kilamanjaro+

Malindi

TANZANIA

Mombasa
Diani
Beach

IN